BUY*i*NG
BREAKFAST
for my
KAM*i*KAZE
P*i*LOT

BUY*i*NG
BREAKFAST
for my
KAM*i*KAZE
P*i*LOT

~

POEMS BY NORMAN STOCK

SALT LAKE CITY

First Edition

97 96 95 94 93   5 4 3 2 1

This is a Peregrine Smith Book, published by Gibbs Smith, Publisher
P.O. Box 667, Layton, Utah 84041 (801) 544-9800.

Design by Kathleen Timmerman

Cover illustration by Cary Henrie

Dawn Valentine Hadlock, Editor

Printed and bound in the United States of America

Library of Congress Cataloging-in-Publication Data
Stock, Norman, 1940–
    Buying breakfast for my Kamikaze pilot : poems / by Norman Stock.
— 1st ed.
      p. cm. — (The Peregrine Smith poetry series)
    ISBN 0-87905-601-0 : $9.95
    I. Title. II. Series.
PS3569.T586B68 1994
811′.54—dc20
                         94-4868
                         CIP

For Lydia

ACKNOWLEDGMENTS

These poems first appeared in the following publications:

ASYLUM ANNUAL: "Spring"

BROOKLYN REVIEW: "Wallace Stevens Sleeping"

COLLEGE ENGLISH: "The Broken Doorbell," "Change of Plans," "Chicken Love," "The Dead Horse of Poetry," "Duck Hunting," "The First Time I Robbed Tiffany's," "The Funeral," "A Giant Woman is Talking to Me," "How to Get Out of Bed," "The Insect Conspiracy," "The Man with the Skewered Lip," "Nursery," "The Stone House," "This Must Be My Stop"

DENVER QUARTERLY: "Summarizing A Lost Notebook"

HANGING LOOSE: "On Faith"

NEW ENGLAND REVIEW AND BREAD LOAF QUARTERLY: "My Uncle's Pajamas," "The Power of Prayer"

NEW YORK QUARTERLY: "Do You Want a Chicken Sandwich," "Free Gift from the Bank," "The Innocent," "Thank You for the Helpful Comments"

POET LORE: "Homeless"

WHEREAS: "My Problem"

CONTENTS

I

II

III

I

The First Time I Robbed Tiffany's

The first time I robbed Tiffany's it was raining. And it was dark, and the wind was blowing. It was like the first time I had sex. The same kind of weather, the same kind of feeling. Me and the girl in the car. Just like me and the cop in the car, after he arrested me outside the store in the rain. I promised myself I would do better next time. Just like I promised the girl. Just like I promised the cop. It felt like it always felt, me and the cop, me and the girl, me and the rain, and the wind and the darkness, and the robbery I never committed, the sex I never had, the girl I never knew, the feel I never copped, and the rain the rain the rain was all I knew and all I will ever know.

The Stone House

two men walk by me
one carries a rope
the other one holds an axe
they say nothing to me they only walk by
but I am curious I follow them
they go to a stone house in my old neighborhood
they walk up a back stairway I follow them
at the top of the stairs they turn and see me walking up
     the stairs toward them
he is coming, one of them says
we meet in a small room they tie me up
the axe is not to be used, I am told, only the rope
then what is the axe for, I say, if not to be used on me
it was to get you to follow us, I am told, so we would
     have you here
what is to become of me, I say, and there is an odd
     confidence in my voice
you will remain as you are, I am told, your life will
     not be any different than before
I know, I say, I have always known that, and I have
     always been like this, but never here
you are wrong, I am told, this is where you have always
     been
in this stone house, the only difference is that we are
     here with you now

The Power of Prayer

I woke up and was surrounded by rabbis
there was a rabbi in the bathtub
there was a rabbi in the sink
there was a rabbi lying on the floor of the kitchen
I knew this would happen someday, I said
what can I do, what can I do
I should have been prepared
as usual, I waited for the last minute
and now the rabbis are all over the place
I peeked into the living room
two rabbis were seated opposite each other drinking tea
o my god, I said, more rabbis
maybe I can hide in the closet, even for a moment, just
    to get some relief
so I opened the closet, and there were rabbis hanging
    from the hangers
holy shit, I said, this is worse than I thought
I ran to the door, and I knew that by this time the
    rabbis had noticed me
I opened the door and almost bumped into the biggest
    rabbi I ever saw in my life
I am the biggest rabbi you ever saw in your life, he
    said
you're damn tootin', I said, hey, can you get me out of
    here
are you kidding, he said, can't you see, I'm one of them
yeah, but you're talking to me, I said
sometimes we talk, sometimes we listen, but we are still
    rabbis, he said, and you will never escape
I dodged him and got to the elevator
naturally the elevator was full of rabbis
in the street I ran to the police station
it had been taken over by rabbis
finally I did the only thing I could think of
I went to the synagogue, I wanted to pray
the synagogue was full of my neighbors and friends
what are you all doing here, I said
we came here to escape the rabbis, they said, they have
    taken over the neighborhood
we all prayed, we prayed for hours and hours, and when I
    went home it was like a miracle
all of the rabbis were gone, not a trace of them left
thank god, I said, thank god, my prayers have delivered
    me from rabbis

Burned Alive

the fire starts while I am sleeping
it surrounds my bed where I am dreaming of plastic
    animals
it nibbles at the sides of my forehead hair by hair
when I wake up I am not surprised
my long-standing identity crisis is over I am being
    burned alive
this is what I always wanted this is destiny
when I scream you will not come running with pails of
    water
no let the fire eat me I am so happy
it is better to be burned alive than to be sleeping
and then to wake up and not to see a fire

How to Get Out of Bed

here's how
you get out of bed
you get out of bed
like this
one foot at a time
one leg at a time
one life at a time
and you're up
but that's only the beginning
then you have to drag your whole godforsaken body
up from the dead of the sleeping
and into the light of the world
fuck it I think I'll crawl under
the covers and stay where I am
which doesn't mean I don't know how to get out of bed
it's actually just like I said one foot at a time one leg at
    a time one life at a time and you're up but that's
    only the beginning

On Faith

the rabbi in my head
went for a long walk
he met a woman by the water
he lifted her up
he said, I am tired of walking
let's lie down
but you are a rabbi, she said
not anymore, he said
I was a rabbi once
now I believe in the grass
but you can't just stop being a rabbi, she said
I have stopped, he said, you will have to take it
    on faith

The Innocent

I must look safe
the nun sits next to me
she doesn't know what I am thinking
chinese girls fucking roosters
could she think of that
great vaginas blossoming mammoth mushrooms
the availability of women
how could she know
I look so safe
go ahead, sister
sit next to me

A Giant Woman is Talking to Me

A giant woman is talking to me. She is telling me about my mistakes, how I have ruined everything.

"But listen," I say, "is it really that bad?"

"It is worse than you think," she says, "worse even than I am saying."

"Then how bad is it?" I ask.

"Your mistakes are as bad as I am big," she says. And she shifts her giant body, almost knocking me over with her massive hip.

"It's okay," I say, "I will fix it all up, I will make things right."

She stares down at me, and I can see by the look in her enormous eyes that she does not think I can do it. Then she slowly rises, a mountain that is beginning to move.

"Wait," I say, reaching up and almost touching her huge hand that is spread above me like a canopy. But she pulls her hand away and continues rising up. "Is there no use?" I say.

"None," she says. And as she turns to leave, the wind of her turning hits me so hard I lose my balance and am soon rolling on the ground.

"Will you be back?" I scream out, regaining my footing. But she is already far away. "Will you help me?" I yell. But all I have left is her absence, as large as my life.

This Must Be My Stop

A train is in motion and I am holding on under it. The train is speeding through a tunnel and I have to hold on tight or I will be killed. I am holding on tight and then the train turns into a huge dog and I am holding on to it. I have to hold on tight or I will be killed. I am holding on tight but then the dog drops me.

I am killed.

I get up off the ground and reach into my pocket. I still have the train ticket. The ticket has a picture of a dog on it. I look closer and I see writing on the ticket. It says, "this ticket entitles you to be killed."

I throw the ticket away.

Who needs this shit.

The Funeral

I don't know what to wear to the funeral, so I go naked. Nobody notices me, everyone is so busy looking at the coffin and crying. An old woman nudges me with her elbow. "Why aren't you crying," she says, "are you made of stone?"

"Why should I cry," I say, "I don't even know who died."

"Then what are you doing here," she says, "who invited you?" And she begins to look around for someone in authority to usher me out.

"Listen lady," I say angrily, "for all you know, I'm the most important person here."

She eyes me suspiciously. Suddenly a look of fear comes into her face. "You're naked!" she screams.

Everything stops. There is a silence as the people turn to look at me. "He's naked!" everyone starts shouting, surrounding me as if to somehow cover me with their bodies.

"Wait!" I say, "wait! None of this excitement is necessary. I am no different than the rest of you. I just didn't know what to wear, that's all."

"Look in the coffin!" somebody yells. And the crowd moves toward the coffin while two of them hold me back. It's hard for me to see what's going on, but I peek between the two men holding me and I see the coffin being opened. To everybody's surprise, it turns out to be empty. Then I am flung forward and thrown in the coffin.

"This is all a terrible mistake," I say, but the lid is closed with a finality that convinces even me. Then I notice how comfortable it is in the coffin and it does seem right for me to be there. Nestling myself in, I listen to the music, I hear singing, I feel good. I realize why I have come to the funeral. I know what it is all about. I lie back happy, dressed as I am.

All

I am all I ever was
in between each breath I breathe
and the sunlight and the sun
I am all I ever was
in between the dark and dark
I am all I ever was
though the sun be caught and tried
and the waters wiped away
I am all I ever was
in between the eye and eye
I am all I ever was
though the earth be turned to dust
and the clouds be scattered, lost
I am all I ever was

Nothing to Worry About

I don't want to be home when the executioner comes, so I conspire to be someplace else. I ask a friend to hide me, knowing he will refuse. Then I buy a ticket to a movie, but I do not go. When the executioner rings my bell, it turns out that I am lying on the bed in my room reading a book about spelling reform, but the executioner does not know this. He assumes I have been hidden by a friend or have gone to the movies. His ringing of my doorbell is strictly routine, like a salesman making his rounds.

I decide to fake him out and answer the door. He is so dumfounded to see me standing there, he almost drops his axe. "Here," I say, catching it in my hand before it slips entirely from his grasp, "you don't want to lose this."

The executioner burns with silent anger to see me there, and is even more angry at my helping him to hold on to his axe. "You idiot," he says, "what makes you think you're so safe from me? You were supposed to be hidden by a friend or gone to the movies, not waiting for me like a lamb for the slaughter." And as he rages at me he once again loses his grip on the axe, which I eagerly help him to secure, placing it firmly in his grasp.

"There is so much of this I can take!" he thunders, the spittle beginning to spout out of his mouth all over his ferocious black beard.

"You're disgusting!" I say. "Wipe your mouth, please. And kindly hold on to your axe, and would you mind stating your business clearly instead of standing here hemming and hawing. It was, after all, *you* who rang *my* doorbell."

"I have come to finish you off," he says, "but your impudence is positively excruciating to my sense of myself as an executioner. I absolutely refuse to deal with you under these conditions!" And he turns to go, a disappointed elephant who has lost his little peanut.

"Well, awright." I say, imitating an outmoded hippie jargon. "hey, man, if you don't wanna play the game, then you'll have to get wet in the rain."

And off he goes, thundering some crazed executioner's oaths, as he waddles away dragging his axe.

Such a dodo, I think, maybe I should have gone to the movies after all. And I wander back to my bed, picking up where I left off with the latest in spelling reform. Again the doorbell rings, but this time I do not answer. I have had enough of executioners for one day, and who knows, it might be one of those infernal salesmen or, even worse, a Jehovah's Witness. I definitely refuse to answer the door, no matter how hard or persistent the ringing.

When the axe comes crashing through the door, I simply bury my head deeper into the book I am reading. I never knew spelling reform could be so interesting. Hearing the door being hacked to pieces, I realize it must be the executioner again, this time more determined to get me, but I know that once he sees me lying on the bed waiting for him, he will again be exasperated and leave. As for the door, well, I can always get a new one. Nothing to worry about.

Change of Plans

delivered myself to the executioner at 8 am sharp he was busy so I left came back at 3 pm executioner still busy so I left again things were getting out of hand went down to the bakery bought some bread ate it went back to see if the executioner would ever be in was told not to return till sent for went home angry what do you have to do to get to see him went to a very boring party got stuffed with cheese and crackers went home sick of myself who I was as if I would be this way forever dialed the executioner's number and as soon as the receiver on the other end was off the hook yelled as loud as I could fuck you you slimy bastard and hung up with a crash felt exhilarated ran immediately out and took a long ride on the subway with all the other sleepy people feeling glad to be with them went home happy fell into bed and when the executioner called got up put my clothes on and instead of going to see him walked away in a totally different direction

The Truth About Me

Actually, I'm a buffalo. I only walk around in the body of a man, the part of me that people can see. But inside, the buffalo that I am remains, holding me heavily to the earth. When I walk fast, my buffalo body lumbers behind me, calling me back. If I choose to listen, it is almost the way it used to be, but not quite. Much as I would like to, I cannot stay that way for long. Soon I get caught up in the world and I must leave my buffalo body behind. While I sleep, of course, I lie down real close to him, but never as close as I once was, long ago.

There was a time when I was happier when I was all buffalo. Then I went through the world unencumbered. But the human part of me grew, somehow, from the part of my buffalo-being that was tired of what it was. Now the human part has become tired of itself and looks longingly at the buffalo that it once was.

I'm very sad about this whole thing, but there is nothing much I can do about it now. My human self is intractable, a brickwork with no openings. This is in sharp contrast to the buffalo I was and still am, somewhere deep inside. Then I was warm and loving, I was an animal with the other animals. But you can't be a buffalo forever, just as you can't be human forever.

Someday this will change. I look forward to that day as I watch the buffalo I was sleep in the person I am, lumbering behind where I can just about feel his breath. O, lovely animal, stay where you are! I don't really want you back, for all of your supple strength. I need something different now, something neither animal nor human. But what can one expect, after being a buffalo and becoming human, is there anything else?

II

The Dead Horse of Poetry

I beat it with my black whip
I hit it so hard it cried neigh neigh as horses cry
then I kicked it because I love to kick it and it
      grovelled at my feet
this poetry this nothing this dying this whimpering
      horse
I put my hand in its mouth and it didn't even bite

I'm Feeling Fine. And You?

cut glass won't help
bald headed bakers won't help
mosquitoes flying in and out of mosquito nets won't help
the seltzer truck won't help
your grandfather with his hands in his overalls won't help
not thinking of blue monkeys won't help
nothing will help
die already die already nothing will help

Homeless

he said he wanted to stay in the apartment
I said look dad to stay here alone you have to be able to
    take care of yourself
and you can't do that anymore so you will have to go to
    the home
I don't want no home he said I want to keep my apartment

so he went to the home and I said isn't this better
you don't have to struggle to stay alive they give you your
    meals they take care of you
I hate it he said I want to go home and he piled his clothes
    on the bed
listen I said you go home to your godamn apartment and
    you will never see me again
and I left and he went home the old coot where he couldn't
    take care of himself

where he drove away the people hired to help him and made
    it impossible for anyone to do anything for him
where he wandered the streets and acted funny and ate
    twenty six meals a day and slept and slept and slept
    and generally made a mess of everything
finally he was back in the home then back in the apartment
    then back in the home again this time for good

I visit him on saturdays I say you are doing fine
I hate it he says but I will stay awhile if you insist
we go for a walk we have coffee he says he enjoys the visit
the days go the nights go he is in the home and he hates it
after a few years he gets sick his leg hurts his arteri-
    osclerosis has him and then he dies

now I think of his grave and the stone and the homelessness
    he never wanted
here on the lonely earth where we would not take him in
because of his old age craziness and his homelessness begs
    me to look at him
to see that he wanted a home but his craziness drove away
    everyone
here on the homeless earth where the final home is a stone
    and the bed of the grass

Nursery

it must be that the mouth must
be something that a newborn kid must
want to have something in all the time
in order not to feel far away
and without anything it must be that it must
take ages to get over this it must
hurt to have to give up always getting
something in the mouth that the mouth needs
that the kid needs that it needs
all the time it must be impossible
to ever forget this it must be murder
to remember it must be murder to remember

Do You Want a Chicken Sandwich

the time my mother opened the door
to the living room and saw me on my knees
with my hard cock in my hand jerking off
in front of the television set with a hot magazine at my side
and she gasped and quickly shut the door
but she did finish what she started to say
when she first pushed it open which was
do you want a chicken sandwich
okay I probably said to the door and put my cock back in my pants
and went and ate my chicken sandwich
while in the next room through all of this embarrassment
my father was playing the violin always the same old song

Chicken Sandwich Nissy

they called me chicken sandwich nissy
nissy for my real name nissen which I changed to norman
and chicken sandwich because of the story of the chicken
    sandwich
when my mother caught me jerking off and asked me what I
    wanted to eat
naturally I had to tell my friends about it
and here I am now norman but deep inside
I am and will always be who I was then chicken sandwich
    nissy
caught with the hot goods in my hand and hungry and
    humping and here

Thank You for the Helpful Comments

I sit quietly listening
as they tear my poem to shreds in the poetry workshop
as each one says they have a "problem" with this line
      and they have a "problem" with that line
and I am not allowed to speak because that is the
      etiquette of the workshop
so I sit listening and writhing while they tear the guts out
      of my poem and leave it lying bleeding and dead
and when they're finally finished having kicked the
      stuffing out of it
having trimmed it down from twenty lines to about four
      words that nobody objects to
then they turn to me politely and they say well Norman
      do you have any response
response I say picking myself up off the floor and brushing
      away the dirt while holding on for dear life to what I
      thought was my immortal poem now dwindled to nothing
and though what I really want to say is can I get my money
      back for this stupid workshop what I say instead is . . .
      uh . . . thank you for your helpful comments . . .
      while I mumble under my breath motherfuckers
      wait till I get to *your* poems

The Man with the Skewered Lip

A man with a skewered lip enters a train. People look away, they don't want to be caught staring. The man sits down, opens a newspaper, and begins reading, covering his face with the paper. People stare at the newspaper, since it is now safe to stare. Suddenly the man lowers the newspaper and looks at the people staring at him. "Is this what you want to see?" he says, pointing to his skewered lip.

The people on the train are embarrassed. They look away again. Each one wants to blame the other for the staring, as if to say, it wasn't me, it was my neighbor who made me do it. The man with the skewered lip looks accusingly at them, one by one. Then he takes the skewer out of his lip, points it at one of the passengers, and says, "Do you want it now?"

The passenger says no, what would he do with it. "You put it in your lip" says the man, doing just that. "See," he says, "you all want to stare, but which one of you dares to skewer your lip as I have done? Not one of you has the nerve to become what you stare at in fascination, not one of you will ever be as I am." With that, he turns back to his newspaper, covering his face as he lifts it to read.

Rovner

Rovner was an annoyance to my family
a violinist with twisted fingers he used to come up
to watch television with us or play the violin with my father
    but most of all to talk
to tell us about the awful culture of America
he must have been a lonely man he was fifty or so and lived
with his parents and never worked or anything an old fellow-
    traveller a communist from the days of the communists
his teeth were rotting but he sure could play the violin
even with the twisted fingers of his right hand from an
    accident
which was his excuse for not having become a great violinist
once when Rovner was in our house he started talking while
    we were all watching television
and my mother said please Mr. Rovner I am watching
    television
and Rovner stopped talking and after a while he said it's been
    a pleasure being a guest in your home these many
    evenings
and he left and never came back and my father said that
    Rovner must have been insulted
but when my father said this he kind of laughed as if to say
    the guy's a nut anyway as we all know
but we still would meet him on the street he liked to walk
    with me and my father and rant on and on
about America me and my friends would laugh at him the
    way he looked
and talked so seriously even to us didn't he know all we
    wanted to do was have fun and laugh
at jerks like him or did he sense some secret bond between
    himself and us
once I told him I liked Florian Zabach the Liberace of the
    violin and Rovner said no
the difference between Florian Zabach and Heifetz he said
    was in the control that Heifetz had
oh I said but I never did forget that I have to hand it to
    Rovner
he really did show me the difference between art and kitsch
    with that one word control
and with his rotting teeth his constant rant his pure old
    fashioned lonely funniness he sure could play the violin

My Uncle's Pajamas

my uncle wears white pajamas
he is with my aunt who is naked
they lie awake in the same bed
my uncle has trouble falling asleep
my aunt drinks coffee and looks at him
sometimes they pace the room together
then they lie down
she lies next to him
touching his white pajamas
he does not touch her
and he cannot fall asleep
he says, you and your coffee
will keep us both awake for years
sleep, she says, sleep, sleep
no, he says, not in my white pajamas
I have put them on only to lie next to you, not to sleep,
        because I wanted to touch you, not to sleep
now I must drink my coffee, she says, and they both lie
        there awake
he not touching her and both of them refusing to sleep

how do you like my uncle
what do you think of my aunt
how do you like my uncle's white pajamas
do you think he should wear yellow pajamas
do you think if he wore yellow pajamas he would do better
what do you think of my aunt being naked
do you think she drinks too much coffee
do you think she should sleep more
could it be that what matters most about all of this are the
        white pajamas my uncle is wearing

aunts and uncles and how they sleep and how they don't sleep
is that what poetry is about is that why I lie awake and look
        at the darkness
imagining them, what they wear and what they don't wear
        and how they touch and don't touch as they both lie
        awake in my mind
while I look at the darkness and I see my uncle's white
        pajamas and I see my naked aunt
and I invent them while I stare at the darkness that is
        everybody's uncle in his white pajamas and everybody's
        aunt drinking coffee and refusing to sleep
is that what poetry is about staring at the darkness staring
        at my uncle's white pajamas staring at my naked aunt

Wallace Stevens Sleeping

There is a commotion in the parlor
The couch is covered with green silk

A black suited figure slouches in it
A cigar dangles from his hand

He is dreaming of the sea that surrounds us every day
He is thinking: the winds rise, and no one notices

Do not wake him, let him lie
Lost in his dreams, soon he will think of us.

The Wallace Stevens Method of Selling Insurance

Wallace Stevens, famous magician and comedian
has come to town to talk about insurance

but nobody wants to buy they want poetry
I don't know from poetry says Wallace Stevens

and he pulls a rabbit out of his shirt
and he tells the one about the travelling salesman

and the farmer's daughter and we laugh so hard
he's such a card this Wallace Stevens that finally we
      even buy his insurance

Chicken Love

looking in the dark
and seeing only chickens

when the darkness envelops chickens
will there be any light left

a darkness in which there are no chickens
this will be the last darkness

the last chicken you will see
will come at you, out of that darkness

Duck Hunting

I.

I put on my duck hunting hat, the one with the ear flaps, and go out to hunt ducks.

It is raining cats and dogs, and there is not a duck in sight.

II.

If you see a duck, shoot. If you hear a shot, duck. Will this rain never stop?

III.

Bang! I shot a duck.

No. I missed. That's life.

IV.

I duck under a tree for shelter. The tree is shaped like a huge duck. I vow never again to go out to hunt ducks.

V.

Is that a duck I see flying?

No. It was only a stone in the air.

A madness of ducks has come over me. I am positively burning to see a real duck.

VI.

Through the rain, I saw a small duck sitting on the water. But when I approached it was not a duck at all, only the shadow of a large leaf.

I cursed myself and my whole life's history. Why was I fated to go duck hunting in the rain?

VII.

The duck hunts me. I am its prey. And I *will* be caught.

My gun lies untended on the rainy earth and I have gone to live with the invisible ducks of the forest and the pond.

It is better this way. Not to hunt, but to live with the hunted, and to float upon the surface of the water, till I must, as all ducks must, fly away forever.

My Problem

I fell in love with a character out of a novel
And we diddled and dawdled together it was ridiculous

To be so much in love what an affair I thought it would
    never end
The way we were always climbing all over each other
    groping and slurping

With finger and tongue I thought I would never forget her
Or get over her after all it went on for nearly twenty years

What a novel! I'm still writing it chapter by chapter and
    book by book
When will it ever end the story is over but I keep describing
    the characters the way they look one has a hook-nose
    and one has a beautiful face and right in the middle of
    everything that great love affair of mine but it's the best
    thing I ever had going for me and I don't know how to
    end it

My White Wife

my white wife
looks at me funny, and says, when will you change
I can't help it, I say, I have always been like this
although I never noticed it, until I met you
I am not white, she says, and you are not black
as usual, you have exaggerated the situation till it is
        impossible for us to talk
but we *are* married, I say, you and I and all the others
the others? she says, there you go again
oh, you know what I mean, I say with a cunning smile
get lost, she says, please get out of my life
so soon? I say, out! she says, away! I am not married to
        anyone
then I will take my blackness, I say, taking my blackness
and I will go with it to another, and I will never come back
good riddance! she says happily, and you can take my
        whiteness with you, since only you can see it
thank you, I say, but I will need another white wife, the
        embodiment not just the quality
you and your fantasies! she says contemptuously, go already,
        go, please, go
all right, I say, all right, I'm going, but you will be sorry
        someday
there was something in it for you, too, you know
but already she has forgotten me, has turned away so
        completely I can barely see her standing there
and suddenly I am no longer black and she is no longer
        white and nothing exists except the space we stand in
this is worse than I thought it would be, I say, but it is also
        better, considering what could have happened, I
        guess it's time to move on

Buying Breakfast for My Kamikaze Pilot

she always takes us down for a crash landing
I don't know why she does it
am I the enemy is she
it's hard to tell on this particular morning
but I buy her breakfast anyway I give her all I have
and she gives me all she is whether in anger or love
as we go crashing through the breakfast plates upsetting
    the orange juice and eggs
and the coffee shop becomes our battleground where we
    both die together holding on to each other for dear
    sweet fucking life

My Hyena

guards the gate and will not let me in
holds a heavy lamp against me drives away the flies
defends the flowers keeps the dogs at bay
my hyena is the jackal of the garden and the angel of my
    kitchen wall
the mouse is scared away the roaches run amuck from her
she sprays the wind that kills she wields a mighty garden
    hose
my hyena keeps all things in place and she is sure to wash
    the grime of years
for in her wake no little creatures stir and all the work of
    men is torn and lost
with my hyena I am fixed and quiet all my days are numbed
    and spent
the flux of years is gone the riot quelled of sense and every
    little life is saved for good
for my hyena wants that nothing dies and only in her sight
    can flowers live
that from her careful watch will not escape nor me myself
    her surly bite

The Broken Doorbell

the broken doorbell rings interminably in my mind
it is the nipple of consciousness, that I want to put my
  mouth around
no, it is the cunt of circumstance, I have to meet her
  somehow
no, it is my own hope for myself, broken again and again
  by the resplendent fingers of the morning
no, it is you, squashed into a little hat with a button to
  squeeze and strum
no, it is not you, how could it be you, this is totally
  ridiculous, of course it isn't you
it is you, the broken doorbell is you, you are ringing my
  chime
I told you I was right, can't you hear me, what's the matter,
  can't you hear me
no, okay, forget it, I will go away forever, and the doorbell
  will be broken for real
no, no, no, it is you, it is you, I'm telling you, it is you
you are coming into my room with your wires hanging out
  with your mechanism unplugged
you are eating me alive with your brokenness you are
  ringing in my head without a stop

Spring

The barber is dreaming of spring, sharpening his scissors. Will spring never come, he muses, and will I always be a barber? A man with a red beard comes in to have his beard trimmed and the barber goes to work on him. "Your red beard reminds me of spring, and that I am destined to be a barber forever," says the barber, as he trims the man's beard.

"Nothing has to go on forever," says the man with the red beard. "You can be whatever you want to be, take it from me."

The barber finishes trimming the man's beard and then locks up the shop. He goes with the red-bearded man up to the corner, where the man points to a house a few blocks away. The barber goes to the house and rings the doorbell. There is no answer, so he goes around the side, forces a window open, and climbs in. The house is practically empty, there is very little furniture, but it contains many rooms. The barber gets down on his hands and knees and leaps from room to room like an animal, bouncing off the walls and clattering up to the ceiling.

In the evening, the red-bearded man comes into the house and sees the barber bounding about. He pats the barber's head and puts a chain around his neck. Then he takes the barber out for a walk to show him off.

"This is my barber," he says to his friends who stoop to admire the leaping thing at his side.

"What a beautiful animal," the people say, patting the barber on the head.

When they return to the house, the red-bearded man lies down to sleep and the barber curls up by his side. Flowers are blooming in the windows of the house and the grass has grown outside almost overnight. It is spring in the world of the barber and in the world of the red-bearded man.

The Demon

A demon spun out of control and fell right out of hell. As he fell he rose upward and entered my life. This particular demon was, of course, no ordinary demon. For one thing, he carried a crooked stick, and for another thing, he continually spoke to me in a language I could not understand.

"Take your stick and go," I said to the demon, "you are a great trouble to me."

"I cannot go," said the demon. "I have been sent here to talk to you in a language you will never understand."

It was impossible to get rid of him, especially since his stick was twirled around my left leg at one end and his right arm at the other.

"Stupid imp," I would say to him, "why must you entangle me with your ridiculous stick like this?"

"It is all I have to hold you," said the demon, "since you cannot understand me when I speak."

This went on for many years until one day I stepped free of him. It was incredibly delightful not to have the stick wound around my leg and not to have to listen any-more to his idiotic ravings in a language I could never understand. My freedom lasted about three days, then, gradually, I began to miss the demon.

"Where are you?" I finally said, feeling like I was giving in to a longing that was greater than any freedom I could ever feel.

"Right here," said the demon, quickly placing the end of the crooked stick around my leg. "I have, after all, been here all along. You're stepping free of me was only an illusion."

"Listen wise guy," I said, "let me tell you at least one thing. I now know how to get out of your grasp. So don't be so sure you have me."

He only smiled and winked his demonic wink, and held his end of the stick firmly, hopping around in a kind of mock dance.

"I got you. I got you," he said spitefully. "I am the demon you need. The one you will never understand."

"Yeah, yeah," I said, humoring him, although I must say I liked the feel of the curl of his crooked stick around my leg. It was something I could be sure of. But what was beginning to bother me was that I felt like I sort of understood him for the first time. I knew this might be dangerous, because if he found out, I was sure he really would leave me.

"You and your silly games," I said. "Think you know all about me, don't you?" And I winked my human wink at him, holding him just where he was.

Free Gift from the Bank

I would like to open an account with you
yes you putting your tits on the table
for my eyes to see yes and enter
my name here of course and I want
the iron as a gift and you sign
my account and me put my name here
between your tits on the table and no
I am not married or henpecked and yes
my cock needs a place to wedge itself in and yes
you will do fine is that it then all right
in two weeks I will expect the iron

The Insect Conspiracy

so I powdered the insects
the way I did it was I opened their bodies
and poured the powder in, then I put them in the box
with the others, where they all whispered together

II.

my dreams are so simple, obvious even
the way I handle too much and can't handle anything at all
am run over by everyone while I make sure it is all in place
taking care of the particulars, never losing anyone or
     winning anything

III.

to stop dreaming and start living is the most ancient of hopes
when I first devised this method, did I know where it would
     lead
and now even the insects are conspiring against me
though I have powdered them carefully, and put them away
     where they belong

The Salesman

The salesman insisted that his set of Bible illustrations was the most original and valuable ever produced. "I know the artist myself," he said, "a monk in the Himalayas. He eats only weeds, drinks green tea, and his spiritual nobility shines through clearly in these pictures. You need this work."

I leaned back and examined the prints. They looked like cheap cartoons sketched on the kind of cardboard used by Chinese laundries to keep shirts stiff. "I don't know much about art," I said quietly.

"The works of a master," said the salesman proudly, "and I am offering them to you at a fantastic pre-publication price. As an investment, you can't go wrong on this. Even if you don't like the pictures."

"That's right," I said finally, after staring at them a little longer, "I don't like the pictures."

"But as an investment," he said, shaken by my negative response, "you stand to gain eventually."

I looked at him as if he was something the rain had washed in, the merest old beggar cluttering my doorway. "I have never invested in art, and I'm certainly not going to start with these pictures," I said with a snort.

"So you don't like me," said the salesman, cowering beneath my glance, his sample illustrations trembling in his grasp.

"You?" I said, looking down at the card he had dropped on my desk, "you? John Junk Petersen, sales representative of the Amalgamated Bible Illustration Corporation. You? I have no opinion at all about you. As for your pictures, they are pure shit."

Dropping his sample case, the salesman bent down on the floor to pick it up. But the next moment, he was grovelling at my feet, begging for another chance, to show me more, to do anything I wanted, anything, whatever would help him make the sale. As he pleaded with me from his position on the floor, he gradually turned into an insect, like one of those large waterbugs that go "splat" when you step on them.

"Splat!" he went when I stepped on him. Kicking him out of my office, I used one of the cardboard pictures as a dustpan to take him out to the garbage. Throwing him into the trash, sample pictures and all, I felt a pang of guilt. Maybe he has a family, I thought.

I went back to my office and noticed that his card was still on my desk, with the phone number of his home office on it. I called and ordered five sets of the pictures, making sure the order was credited to the account of the salesman, who now lay dead in the trash, like the insect he was. Who knows, I thought, maybe there will be a market for these odd illustrations. Bibles have always been popular, and so have Bible pictures. In fact, with the job market the way it is, who knows? What if I lost the job I have now? I could wind up working for his company and then I'd be selling the damn things myself! I put the card in my wallet just in case. After all, with the salesman gone, I knew there would be an opening.

Manhattan

The mice in the coffee shop decide to take it over. They tie up the owner's fingers with little mouse bands and warn him, at peril of his life, to give all his earnings to them. "But how will I live?" he protests.

"You will work for us," the mice say, "we will give you a weekly allowance."

I enter the coffee shop and order my usual breakfast—eggs sunny side up, toast and coffee. But I notice mouse hairs on the whites of the eggs. I call the owner over, demanding to know what these little mouse hairs are doing on my eggs. As he tries to explain what has happened, I notice the mouse bands on his fingers, "What are those?" I ask.

"I've been trying to tell you," he says, "the mice that used to live in the walls of the kitchen have forced me to work for them."

"That's terrible," I say, and I begin to feel frightened.

I quietly eat my eggs, mouse hairs and all, and am in a great hurry to leave without letting on that I know what has happened. As I rise to go, careful to leave a big tip on the table, I feel a slight gnawing at my left foot. Looking down, I see hundreds of mice in formation, ready to get me. I bolt for the door, but am tripped up by the mice, who bind my fingers with little mouse bands and tie an apron around me, forcing me to work for them.

Now I work at the coffee shop with the former owner and the mice watch us carefully. We are never allowed to leave and we must sleep with the mice in the kitchen, but the pay isn't bad. Since mice do not require much, our weekly allowances are quite large. While there are occasional complaints about hair in the food, the business is thriving.

Before I came here I worked in a hat factory. This is a little more confining, but, as I say, the pay is good. The mouse bands are sticky and cut through my fingers sometimes, but it isn't all that bad. The former owner likes my work and the mice also seem pleased. If I can stick it out a little longer, this may all work out very well—I may even become a partner. All in all, I'd say it's been a good job change. Right now I'm taking it one day at a time, but eventually I hope to retire, that is, if the mice will ever let me leave.

Summarizing a Lost Notebook

how April was bad enough not to speak of the perils of
    March
how my life once again sank under my feet because of the
    quicksand of experience
how I labored at the gates of New Jersey and was turned away
    by the blind watchman guarding the suburban wilderness
how they came after me with priestly letters and declaimed
    against me in the professorial marketplace
how the publishers disagreed about me but finally settled it
    all with one vote and their judgement was final
how the rabid secretaries of the office ate me alive drinking
    me down with their morning coffee full of complaints
how the library left me leaning on the porch of expectation
    with my mouth open aching for more
how the she-devil in the closet threw the mothballs at me and
    sent me packing broom in hand
how the furious boss of bosses put a red blanket over my body
    and said he died take him out of here pronto
how it happened all at once when I wasn't looking and now
    they tell me where were you didn't you see the messages
how signs went up all over the city I thought they were
    advertisements but they were really calls to faith and I
    never understood
how I must now keep at it in the streets and subways in the
    buses and taxis how I must keep on moving or be stopped
    in my tracks forever

Murderer's Laughter

The murderer was laughing so hard I could hear him through the window and all the way down the block. Since his laughter was very disturbing, I dialed his number to tell him about it.

"Hello," said the murderer on the other end of the line.

"This is me," I said, "would you mind not laughing so loud."

"I have not been laughing," said the murderer, laughing. "I have been practicing a new form of singing."

"Whatever it is you are doing," I said, "I find it quite disturbing and I would like you to stop it."

"The sound I make is none of your business," said the murderer, "and if you persist in calling me, you better know what may happen to you."

"Is that a threat?" I said, arching my back for a fight. After all, no murderer was going to scare me that easily.

"Just a statement of fact," he said, hanging up.

I took out the Chinese chopper from my kitchen cabinet, put it in a briefcase, and went to pay a call on the murderer. As far as I was concerned, he wasn't going to be practicing his new form of singing much longer.

As I walked up the block with my briefcase, the laughter got louder and louder, reaching an ear-splitting intensity when I arrived at his door. I banged violently on the door, making as much noise as I could. The laughter stopped as the murderer went to open the door. He invited me in, asked me to sit down, and even offered me a drink. I refused the drink, sat down with the briefcase close to me, and began to make my rather reasonable demand.

"Either you stop your ridiculous laughing, or if you want to call it singing, whatever it is, either you stop it, or pay the consequences."

"And what," said the murderer, "are the consequences? Do you not realize that you are talking to a murderer?"

I opened the briefcase and took out the Chinese chopper. Brandishing it in my hand, I rose and stepped toward him. He held his ground, but I could see a shadow of uncertainty clouding his face.

"You are about to be killed," I said, "murderer though you may be."

At first he raised his hands to protect himself, then he started laughing as if what I was about to do was the funniest thing he had ever seen. As I chopped up his face, the laughter continued, but it came out chopped up. This choppy laugh was certainly no less annoying than it had been before, but it grew fainter as the murderer's life left his body. When I finally finished chopping him into little pieces, the laughter was gone and I had a mess to clean up. I found a broom and a dust pan in a closet and, to my surprise, was able to clean up quite easily. Chopped up as he was, he didn't really amount to much. I packed up my chopper and gingerly left the apartment, feeling much better about the whole thing than I had originally, that is, at the beginning of the evening.

Singing indeed! I thought to myself as I walked back down the street, the street that was now so silent you could hear a pin drop. This is the way life should be, I thought, quiet, logical, and finished. Not all this silly laughter and expectation of God knows what. I went up to my place and crawled into bed, happy with myself for the first time in a long time, knowing I had done what had to be done. After all, one less murderer in the world was surely a good thing. The rightness of it all seemed so complete and the silence so fitting that I was overwhelmed with something very much like laughter. In fact, it was as if I was singing for joy as I laughed loudly in my half-sleeping reverie, as if I was practicing some new form of happiness. And if anybody minded my loud laughter, well, let them be damned, for on this night I had become someone to reckon with. I couldn't imagine anyone who would dare to challenge me, and if anyone did, he had better be prepared to pay the consequences. Which is exactly what I told the person who called to complain about my loud laughing. Can't they let me practice my new found joy, this singing, this laughing, in peace?

The Only Survivor

The only survivor made a point of announcing, at each gathering of people he attended, "I am the only survivor."

"How wonderful," people would say, and "how heroic!" But at one such gathering there was a little old lady who insisted on asking over and over, "only survivor of what?" No matter how hard people tried to quiet her down, the old lady persisted in her question. Finally, edging herself through the crowd of his admirers, she found herself face to face with the only survivor himself, to whom she once again asked her question, "only survivor of what?"

"My good lady," said the only survivor, "on what grounds do you dare to ask this impertinent, and as far as I am concerned, totally irrelevant question?"

"On the ground I am standing on, sir" said the little old lady, "which is of course the same ground you are standing on."

"As if it were not enough for a man like me to have lived through what I have lived through," said the only survivor. Needless to say, the crowd of people at the gathering hung on every word he said and looked very much askance at the impertinent little old lady. Who did she think she was, talking to the only survivor like that!

"But sir," said the little old lady, "I only ask to know what it is you have lived through that gives you the right to call yourself extraordinary for having lived through it."

While most in the crowd were still affronted by the little old lady's questioning, some began to turn their heads a little toward the only survivor, as if they too expected an answer to this question which none had ever thought to ask. Feeling this pressure, the only survivor began to shift his weight from foot to foot. "Why many things," he said, "I have lived through so many things . . . "

At this point, the people became aware that the only survivor might indeed be an impostor. They began to look at him with disdain, and some even turned away with disgust. Others took up a more threatening attitude, coming toward him as if to physically punish him for his lies.

"Wait!" said the little old lady, raising her umbrella to stop those threatening him. "I was only asking a question, not making a judgement. Let the man speak."

"All right," said the only survivor, "I will answer the old lady's question, and I will tell the truth. The only thing I have survived is my own life, just as you have all survived yours. So we are all of us only survivors, and it was wrong of me to make of myself a special case. But since I took it upon myself to assume this role, I now, as a kind of penance, bequeath it to all of you." And with that, the only survivor pulled a long knife out of his pocket and plunged it into his heart. He had survived everything before this, but to see his own singularity gone was too much for him. As he lay dead, the people marvelled at the finality of his act, knowing they would have to carry on, each in his own way, the legacy of survival.

The Skin

So I combed my hair with an iron comb, and the skin came off my head. I soaked the skin in oil, stretched it in steam, and I had something I could use against the cold. Good for me, I thought, I have created something worthwhile of myself, no more of this silly passing the time without any good coming of it.

The skin was beautiful, with a sheen to it like the brightest gold. I wore it all the time, mostly over my shoulders, in all kinds of weather. Miraculously, it seemed warm in the cold and cool and soothing when the weather was hot. Only a skin made from one's own body, I thought, could have such wonderful properties.

Then, one day, having hung it on a hook in a restaurant, I went to take it as I left and found it gone. A feeling of having been bereft of something more valuable than my life itself came over me, and I almost banged my head against the wall in anguish at the realization of my own stupidity. How could I have hung my beautiful piece of skin, that I had created myself, on a hook in a restaurant and then have turned my back on it!

When I reported the loss to the police, they only shook their heads into their notebooks. Most robberies are not solved, they said, and your loss is only one among hundreds that occur in the city every day. Besides, said an old wizened cop with a face like a catcher's mitt, who ever heard of losing his own skin. "But that's exactly what happened," I shot back quickly, unfazed by his cruel, professional skepticism.

Well, I thought, giving up on the police, I'll have to get to the bottom of this myself. After all, flesh is flesh, and skin that comes off my own head is more important than anything. I went back toward the restaurant and, sure enough, noticed some fishy-looking characters crouching in an alley nearby. As I approached them, I felt as if I was being encircled in a net, with people closing in on all sides of me. I made a sudden movement to flee, but at the same instant they were upon me and there was no going anywhere. "What is it you want?" I said to the strong arms and bodies now pressed against me and preventing me from escaping.

"Exactly what we were about to ask you," said a rotten tinny voice into my ear.

"I have lost my skin," I said. "It was taken off a hook in the restaurant across the street."

"Your skin was it?" said the same voice, which now seemed to have taken on an Irish lilt. "So it was your skin that was lost?"

"Do you have it?" I asked hopefully, more concerned with getting it back than with any new danger I was in at the moment.

"Have it?" said the voice. "Well, is this it then?" And with a rough gesture, he pushed the skin in my face.

"Yes," I said, "yes," almost fainting with happiness at the feel of it. "Then it was you who took it, and now you are giving it back?"

"Giving it back?" he said, and the other arms that held me took on a firmness, as if I was being held by iron chains. "Did I say anything about giving it back?"

"But surely," I said, noticing that my voice was taking on a disgustingly pleading tone, "surely, now that you have had your fun, you will give me back the skin, after all, it *is* mine."

The loud laughter this evoked in my captors almost knocked me over by the sheer decibel force of it. "Give it back?" they echoed, roaring with yelps of glee. "He says we will give it back!" They laughed so hard that they actually let go of me, and with the skin still on my face, I was able to break away from them. The men who had been holding me bounced back in one body when they saw me leap, but they were not quite fast enough. After all, I now had my skin back, and with it I had a new sureness of movement. Their biggest mistake was to have attempted to mock me by throwing it in my face.

Happier than I ever was before, I wore my skin with pride and walked through the streets like a man made new.

Norman Stock was born in Brooklyn, New York. He received a B.A. from Brooklyn College, an M.L.S. from Rutgers University, and an M.A. in English from Hunter College. He has won several awards for his poetry, including a Bread Loaf Scholarship, Poets and Writers New York to the Heartland Contest, the Writer's Voice New Voice Award, and the Poetry Prize of the Bennington Writing Workshops. His poems have appeared in the *New England Review, College English,* the *New York Quarterly,* and other magazines.

He lives in New York City and is a librarian at Montclair State University in New Jersey.

THE PEREGRINE SMITH POETRY SERIES

Christopher Merrill, General Editor

Sequences, by Leslie Norris

Stopping by Home, by David Huddle

Daylight Savings, by Steven Bauer

The Ripening Light, by Lucile Adler

Chimera, by Carol Frost

Speaking in Tongues, by Maurya Simon

The Rebel's Silhouette, by Faiz Ahmed Faiz
    (translated by Agha Shahid Ali)

The Arrangement of Space, by Martha Collins

The Nature of Yearning, by David Huddle

After Estrangement, by Molly Bendall

Geocentric, by Pattiann Rogers

1-800-HOT-RIBS, by Catherine Bowman

Buying Breakfast for My Kamikaze Pilot, by Norman Stock